LIFEWAYS

The Arapaho

RAYMOND BIAL

BENCHMARK BOOKS

MARSHALL CAVENDISH
NEW YORK

SERIES CONSULTANT: JOHN BIERHORST

ACKNOWLEDGMENTS

This book would not have been possible without the kind assistance of several individuals and organizations who have devoted themselves to preserving the traditions and improving the contemporary life of the Arapaho. I am especially indebted to many helpful people on the Wind River Reservation in Wyoming.

I would like to thank my editor Christina Gardeski for her consistent support and numerous comments in revising *The Arapaho*. I would like to express my appreciation to John Bierhorst for his detailed review of the manuscript, which led to many judicious corrections. As always, I offer my deepest affection to my wife Linda and my children Anna, Sarah, and Luke for their devotion and good company, especially on our exciting trip to Wyoming.

Benchmark Books
Marshall Cavendish
99 White Plains Road
Tarrytown, New York 10591-9001
www.marshallcavendish.com

Library of Congress Cataloging-in-Publication Data
Bial, Raymond.
The Arapaho / by Raymond Bial.
p. cm.—(Lifeways)
Summary: Presents information on the past and present culture of the Arapaho Indians.
Includes bibliographical references and index.
ISBN 0-7614-1684-6
1. Arapaho Indians—History—Juvenile literature. 2. Arapaho
Indians—Social life and customs—Juvenile literature.
[1. Arapaho Indians. 2. Indians of North America—Great Plains.]
I. Title II. Series: Bial, Raymond. Lifeways.
E99.A7B53 2004
978.004'973—dc21
2003008126

Printed in Italy
6 5 4 3 2 1

Photo Research by Anne Burns Images

Cover Photos by Raymond Bial

The photographs in this book are used with permission and through the courtesy of: *Raymond Bial*: 1, 6, 8, 9, 11, 17, 18, 21, 22, 23, 36, 40, 41, 43, 53, 61, 63, 66, 68, 69, 71, 75, 78, 79, 87, 94, 95, 96, 97, 99, 101, 102, 104, 105. *Western History Collection, University of Oklahoma*: 26, 27, 31, 32, 38, 39, 45, 57, 58, 59, 85, 109, 111, 112. *The Philbrook Museum of Art, Tulsa, Oklahoma*: 49. *American Museum of Natural History*: 34 (#31527) Wheelock, 82, 83 (#31528) Wheelock.

This book is dedicated to the Arapaho, who are working to provide a good life for their children and themselves in the Wind River country of Wyoming and on the sweeping plains of Oklahoma.

Contents

Author's Note

AT THE DAWN OF THE TWENTIETH CENTURY, Native Americans were thought to be a vanishing race. However, despite four hundred years of warfare, deprivation, and disease, American Indians have not gone away. Countless thousands have lost their lives, but over the course of the twentieth century the populations of native tribes grew tremendously. Even as American Indians struggle to adapt to modern Western life, they have also kept the flame of their traditions alive—the language, religion, stories, and the everyday ways of life. An exhilarating renaissance in Native American culture is now sweeping the nation from coast to coast.

The Lifeways books depict the social and cultural life of the major nations, from the early history of native peoples in North America to their present-day struggles for survival and dignity. Historical and contemporary photographs of traditional subjects, as well as period illustrations, are blended throughout each book so that readers may gain a sense of family life in a tipi, a hogan, or a longhouse.

No single book can comprehensively portray the intricate and varied lifeways of an entire tribe, or nation. I only hope that young people will come away with a deeper appreciation for the rich tapestry of Indian culture—both then and now—and a keen desire to learn more about these first Americans.

1. Origins

The Northern Arapaho still live on the rolling plains and hills of Wyoming where their ancestors once made their home.

THE ARAPAHO OF WYOMING AND OKLAHOMA—AND FORMERLY COLORADO—
have long called the western plains their home. Rich in tradition, yet
with no written records, the people in earlier times depended on storytelling to help them remember their history. "If we wonder often,"
they said, "the gift of knowledge will come." In the evenings they
would gather around the fire in the tipi and listen as elders related tales
of the past. Here is one story about the flat pipe, the Arapaho's most
sacred object, and how the world came to be:

How the Earth Came to Be

At one time, there was nothing except water on the face of the
earth. A man, woman, and their son floated on a flat pipe for many
days and nights.

One day their son became tired of being confined to the pipe and
said to his father, "I wish you would provide a big place where I could
run and play."

So the father called forth all the waterfowl and stated, "I want you
birds to decide who is the best diver among you. Which of you can
bring soil from beneath the water? My dear boy wishes to live on land."

The waterfowl decided that the duck was the best diver. So the
duck plunged down into the depths of the water. He was gone a long
time and was barely able to touch bottom. When he slowly surfaced,
his eyes were partly closed, but he held a little clay in his webbed feet.

The man took this clay and flung it all around him, declaring that
there should be dry land for them. And some land was formed.

However, the boy said, "My father, this land is too small. I cannot
go far without drowning."

In traditional stories, the Arapaho recount how the hills and valleys of their homeland came to be created out of the vast sea.

So the father called the water turtle and asked him to dive for more clay. The turtle did as he was asked. After a long time bubbles rose to the surface, and the turtle appeared. He had placed a little clay in each of the four hollows in his sides.

The man took the clay and scattered it, asking that more land be formed. And there was land—as far as the eye could see.

The boy was now satisfied. However, the man realized that they needed water on all this land. So he slowly waved the flat pipe in the four directions, and the streams and rivers were formed, all flowing from the foot of the hills and mountains.

The family then went to live on the dry land. This is how the earth was made and how people came to live there.

Early History

Following the herds of buffalo on the northern Great Plains, the Arapaho (pronounced uh-RAP-uh-ho) came to be known as the Bison Path People and by several other names. The term Arapaho may be derived from the Pawnee word *tirapihu*, meaning "trader," or "he who buys or trades." The Arapaho were one of the most renowned trading tribes in the Great Plains region. The name also may derive from a Crow word that means "tattooed people," which is how the Blackfeet referred to the Arapaho. The Cheyenne referred to them as "Cloud Men." The name given to them by the Sioux, "Blue-sky Men," has a similar meaning. Curiously, the Arapaho did not use any of these names. They called themselves *Inuna-ina*, meaning "Our People," or "People of Our Kind."

The Arapaho were one of the few western tribes to speak a language in the Algonquian family of languages. Algonquian languages were more commonly spoken by tribes in eastern North America. In fact, the Arapaho, or their ancestors, once lived in the woodlands around the Great Lakes, near the headwaters of the Mississippi River. There, they must have had many traditions similar to those of other Algonquian-speaking groups, most of whom lived in that region about three thousand years ago. At some point in their long history the ancestral Arapaho began moving onto the Great Plains. In their earliest days they had lived as hunters and gatherers. Eventually they may have settled in semipermanent villages, where they may have grown corn and other crops. Perhaps as late as the early 1700s the people separated. One group turned northward to become the Gros Ventre of Canada and northern Montana, while the other group migrated southward to become the tribe now known as the Arapaho. By the mid-1700s the Arapaho had acquired horses and were rapidly adopting a new way of life—as highly skilled horsemen, buffalo hunters, traders, and raiders. As buffalo hunters, the men worked together to chase down animals and cut them from the herd. With bows and arrows they shot the galloping beasts, which they butchered with flint or bone knives. They took the meat back to camp, where the women cut thin strips, which were then smoked and dried. They scraped and tanned the hides, which were used for making clothing, tipi covers, and many kinds of containers.

As traders, the Arapaho established prosperous relationships with the Hidatsa, Mandan, and other farming tribes who lived in permanent villages along the Missouri River. With these people they most often exchanged packs of dried buffalo meat and cured hides for supplies of corn, beans, and squash. The Arapaho took shelter in tipis. At other times, they raided the camps of their enemies.

Around 1835 the tribe broke into two major divisions, which came to be known as the Northern Arapaho and the Southern Arapaho. According to traditional stories, they split at a winter crossing of the Missouri River when the sheet of ice cracked and each branch went its separate way. However, they also divided because of pressure from settlers who were pushing westward into their hunting territory. The Northern Arapaho roved an area around the North Platte River in present-day Wyoming. The Southern Arapaho lived around Bent's Fort on the Arkansas River, in what is now Colorado. However, both divisions kept in close contact.

The Arapaho often journeyed in the company of the Cheyenne, with whom they had become close allies after encountering them in the Black Hills. The Cheyenne needed the Arapaho as intermediaries in trade with the Missouri River tribes, and both needed each other as warriors against the Crow and other enemies. The Arapaho believed that the creator of the universe, known as Man-Above, had formed the Rocky Mountains as a barrier against their enemies—the Pawnee to the east; the Comanche and Kiowa to the south, along with the Crow; and the Ute and Shoshone in the western mountains.

Spirited and independent, the Arapaho wandered over vast stretches of the Great Plains—from the Cheyenne River into eastern Colorado and

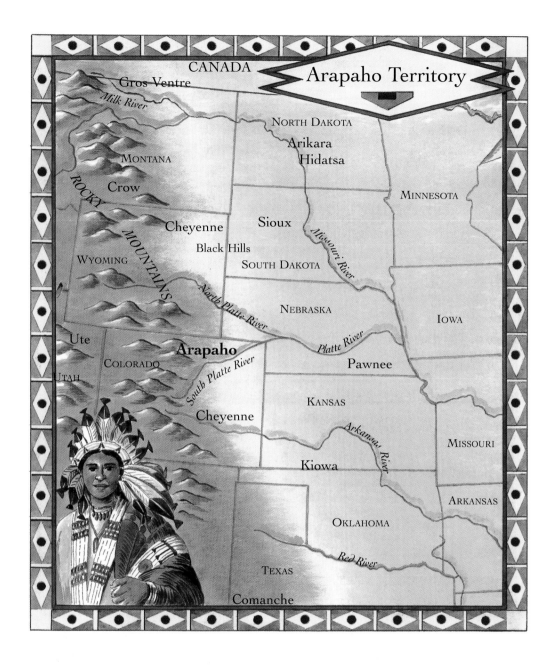

CANADA

Gros Ventre

Milk River

Arapaho Territory

NORTH DAKOTA

Arikara

Hidatsa

MONTANA

ROCKY MOUNTAINS

Crow

MINNESOTA

Cheyenne

Sioux

Missouri River

Black Hills

SOUTH DAKOTA

WYOMING

North Platte River

NEBRASKA

IOWA

Ute

Arapaho

South Platte River

Platte River

COLORADO

Pawnee

UTAH

Cheyenne

KANSAS

MISSOURI

Kiowa

Arkansas River

ARKANSAS

OKLAHOMA

Red River

TEXAS

Comanche

The Arapaho once lived a nomadic life in a vast territory that encompassed much of the northern plains.

from the Black Hills of present-day South Dakota to the Rocky Mountains. While hunting buffalo they might venture as far eastward as the rolling grasslands of Kansas and Nebraska. During the winter they camped in the eastern Rockies along clear, cold streams, keeping warm by their fires as the snows deepened around them. Around 1800 between 3,000 and 5,000 Arapaho ranged over the Great Plains. Although they had rarely encountered European trappers and traders over the years, their way of life would soon be changed forever.

The People and the Land

May this young man, with his people and his relatives, do well, walking where it is good, obtaining food and clothing and horses of many colors, and where there are birds that are crying and the day is long and the wind is good!

—Arapaho prayer on behalf of a young man

When the Arapaho had become skilled horsemen and buffalo hunters, they were able to make use of a territory that extended over 100,000 square miles. Shared with the Cheyenne, Sioux, and other tribes, this vast range mostly encompassed the plains and foothills of eastern Colorado, the southeastern portion of Wyoming, and parts of western Kansas and Nebraska.

In some parts of Arapaho territory, creeks went dry and watering holes blistered in the sun. Only on rare occasions when the clouds thickened and grew black did it rain. A few areas where the Arapaho camped, such as the Black Hills and the Yellowstone country of north-

*T*he Arapaho journeyed great distances in pursuit of the enormous herds of buffalo that once grazed over the Great Plains.

The mountains in Arapaho territory were laced with streams of clear water, which often went dry over the long, hot summer months.

western Wyoming, supported forests and lush carpets of succulent grass and green trees. Rising like islands above the broad plains, these favored areas were cool and full of mysterious shadows. Here there were meadows, slopes blanketed with pines, and clear lakes bordered by spruce, cedar, and aspen trees.

Most of Arapaho territory, however, consisted of a broad swath of the Great Plains, an immense grassland that sprawled from Mexico in the south to Canada in the north. Much of this land was covered with short-grass prairie—little bluestem, buffalo grass, and a sprinkling of flowers—that extended northward from Colorado to the plains of Wyoming. Some stretches of this rolling land were also fragrant with the scent of sage and other herbs used by medicine men in healing rituals. For nearly a century the Arapaho wandered over this vast land that flowed wave upon wave as far as the eye could see. Much of the land was gently rolling or so flat that it appeared to be the floor of the sky. However, the vista was also broken with an occasional ridge buffeted by the wind, mild hills, and low, prominent buttes. Some of the territory was sliced by the gullies and ravines of creek beds. The land rose gradually from east to west to the foothills and then the high ranges of the Rocky Mountains. Often, far into the distance, people could glimpse a jagged row of white-capped peaks.

The Plains were laced by streams, which often went dry, and a few broad, shallow rivers—notably the Platte River in Nebraska and the Arkansas River in Oklahoma. The banks of these streams were fringed with berry bushes, small shrubs, and stands of trees, mostly cottonwoods, whose leaves jangled bright yellow in the autumn. Cattails studded the low, moist ground of marshes and bogs. The Arapaho often camped along these streams, where the clear flowing waters had cut ravines over the ages into the otherwise unbroken land. Here, they had plenty of fresh water and were afforded a little shelter from their enemies and the weather, especially the winds that continually blew over the Plains. If the buffalo herds continued to graze nearby, the band might camp in one spot for several weeks.

The climate of the Plains was marked by four distinct seasons— the bitterly cold winds of winter, the tender green of spring, the bloom of summer, and the golden light of autumn, when leaves and grasses mellowed to various shades of brown. However, the region was especially noted for its extremes of cold and heat. During the brutal winter, especially in the North Country, fierce winds rushed down from the Arctic, bringing numbingly cold temperatures and swirling blizzards. One could easily get lost in the blinding wall of white and quickly freeze to death. By contrast, summers were hot and dry, especially on the southern plains, as the sun beat down on the parched ground. There were occasional droughts during which plants died and streams went dry.

In Arapaho country the Plains received only about fifteen inches of rain each year—mostly from May through June. With this rain, prairie flowers bloomed in a profusion of colors. Later, in the baking heat of summer, many of these plants withered and cast their seeds for next year's blanket of grass and flowers. The infrequent rains usually came as intense storms, with dramatic lightning and thunder and frequently a battering shower of hail. There were often flash floods as the parched gullies and washes quickly filled with rushing water.

Over the spring and early summer, the grasslands often blossomed with small, delicate flowers in many brilliant colors.

*S*treams of blue water branched through the western plains where buffalo grazed on the first tender grass of the summer.

Many animals made their homes in the forests and grasslands of Arapaho territory. Herds of buffalo blanketed the Plains, which they later came to share with droves of wild horses. Swift animals, such as pronghorn antelopes and restless coyotes, also roamed over vast expanses of this territory. Jackrabbits escaped danger in great bursts of speed. Their long ears helped cool them by circulating blood. Beneath the seas of grass were whole towns of prairie dogs, the rodents popping up, then diving back down into their burrows to escape danger and the heat. Lizards, turtles, and snakes eased through the grasses, looking for a little shade. With so few trees prairie chickens and other birds had to tend nests cleverly hidden on the ground while hawks, eagles, and vultures drifted in the sky overhead. Falcons swooped down upon mourning doves, while herons and cranes waded through the shallow water of creeks and streams, which teemed with fish, including carp, sturgeon, and catfish. Ancient paddlefish swam the murky waters of the Missouri River, while trout flashed through mountain streams. Up in the foothills of the Rockies, large game—elk, moose, bighorn sheep, and mule deer—browsed on grass and leaves, always keeping alert for mountain lions, wolves, black bears, and grizzlies. Wild turkeys, partridge, and grouse also flourished among the trees.

As the Arapaho moved seasonally from the Plains to the mountains they made their way into the sheltered valleys and parks of the Rocky Mountains in east-central Colorado. During the fall and early winter the buffalo herds broke up into small groups and scattered widely in these areas, seeking shelter from the intense cold and searching for patches of grass in the snow. Whether there were deep snows or light dustings, the ground froze as hard as iron. Families huddled in their tipis waiting for the spring thaw, when clear waters flowed down streams fringed with ice. When the prairies bloomed with flowers and tender grass, the herds came together again. And the Arapaho once again descended to the plains to begin another yearly cycle of hunting.

2. Camps

The Arapaho lived in tipis that could be
readily set up and taken down as they
followed the herds of buffalo.

ARAPAHO SOCIETY WAS CENTERED AROUND FAMILIES AND BANDS. A HUSBAND and wife and their children occupied a tipi, possibly with an unmarried aunt or uncle and perhaps also a grandparent. Several such family units, each with its own tipi, made up an extended household whose members worked together and shared their food. An older man served as head of the extended household, and his wife was the cook. But everyone helped to care for the children.

Several households made up each of the bands, which lived in temporary seasonal camps as they followed the herds of buffalo. During the winter the bands drifted apart into small groups of families and settled in camps, usually situated along streams. As the snows deepened around them they lived on their stores of dried food—buffalo meat, roots, and berries. Venturing from camp, the men sometimes hunted deer or elk, although game was often scarce during this time of year. On the long winter evenings both children and adults entertained themselves with games, songs, and stories. Or they worked at various crafts, such as chipping arrowheads or making leather pouches. As spring approached, the bands journeyed back onto the open plains and joined the large camps to hunt buffalo and hold ceremonies, the most important of which was the annual Sun Dance. The bands also readily united in warfare.

The bands varied in size, and individuals could move from one group to another, often through marriage. Everyone in the band was considered equal, although a man could achieve prestige based on his wealth, notably the number of horses he owned, and membership in one of the societies, or lodges. Both men and women could belong to one of the lodges, each of which had its own special rites and rules. These shaped the religious, political, and social fabric of the tribe. Arapaho society was structured around eight lodges, ranked by age and ability—two for youths, five for men, and one for women. Each of the societies had its own political and ritual duties.

When they reached a certain age, boys entered the Kit Fox Lodge. After they had proven their skill and bravery, they earned their way into the Star Lodge, then advanced into the men's lodges, from one to another as they grew older. Other men's societies included the Tomahawk, Spear, Crazy, and Dog lodges. Before a man could join the next society, he had to apprentice himself to one of its members and complete special initiation rites. Each society had its own rituals and ceremonies, and its members wore a certain type of regalia. As they progressed through the various societies men gained more prestige and assumed greater responsibilities. The warriors in the Dog Society were known for their honor and courage in battle. Old men who achieved membership in the highest men's lodge enjoyed the highest stature and authority in Arapaho society. The most respected group in Arapaho society was the Water-Pouring Old Men, composed of seven elders who directed lodge ceremonies, cared for the sacred flat pipe, and prayed for the well-being and prosperity of their people. In addition to the men's societies, there was one society for the women. Known as the Medicine Women, or the Seven Old Women, they taught the art of making embroidery and other fine handiwork. A group of shamans, including both men and women, oversaw the lodge rituals, which ensured the survival of the Arapaho.

Traditionally, the Arapaho had no principal chief. Each band had its own leaders, often a peace chief and a war chief. Chosen for his generosity and wisdom, the peace chief was responsible for everyday activities, such as resolving personal disputes, and major decisions, such as breaking camp in the spring. War chiefs were usually members of the Dog Lodge. Chosen for his experience, skill as a hunter, and courage in battle, the war chief took over when the band went on raids. Before the separation into the northern and southern branches, the Arapaho had four (or possibly five) tribal divisions, each of which had its own chief. These chiefs constituted a governing council for the tribe as a whole. Council decisions were made by consensus, meaning that all the members agreed on the action to be taken. After they split into two major groups, the Northern Arapaho and Southern Arapaho each had their own chiefs.

Tipis

Made of wooden poles and sewn buffalo hides, tipis could be quickly set up or taken down in a matter of minutes. Tipis could also be easily transported from one camp to another. The women simply lashed two of the long tipi poles to the shoulders of a dog, and later a horse, to make a V-shaped, sled-like carrier known as a travois (trav-OY) on which they piled the folded tipi covering and their household goods. With the ends of the poles dragging on the ground, a travois worked even better than wheels on the rough ground of the plains.

Chief Circle Left Hand, oldest son of Left Hand, posed for this photograph in full headdress, holding a ceremonial pipe.

A man sits near the doorway of his canvas tipi. Smoke from the cooking fire rose through the open flap at the peak.

Each tipi consisted of wooden poles arranged in a cone shape and sheathed with a covering made of fifteen to twenty buffalo hides. To make the lodge poles for a tipi frame, men cut down long, slender trees and peeled off the bark. The poles were dried in the sun, then hauled back to the camp. To erect a tipi, women first lashed together the tops of three large foundation poles and raised them, spreading out the bottom ends like a tripod as they gradually stood the frame upright. Next, they placed smaller poles in the gaps to complete the frame.

Making a tipi covering was a long and tedious process. Several women spread fresh buffalo hides on the ground and scraped away the fat and flesh. The hides were then stretched and dried in the sun for a few days, after which the shaggy brown hair was scraped away. The women soaked the hides in water to soften them, then rubbed in a mixture of animal fat, brains, and liver. After rinsing the hides in water, they repeatedly worked them back and forth over a rawhide thong until they became pliable buckskin. Finally, the hides were smoked over a fire to give them a tan color. Experienced women oversaw the laying out, cutting, and fitting of the hides. Because of the irregular shape of the hides, this task was like putting the pieces of a puzzle together. Several women then carefully stitched the buffalo hides together.

To sheath the tipi, the covering was attached to a pole, raised to the top, and wrapped around the cone-shaped frame. Held together with wooden pins, the covering had two wing-shaped flaps at the top. When turned back, these flaps left a smoke hole. The flaps

The Arapaho sometimes painted their tipi coverings with bold and colorful designs, which held deep religious meaning.

could be closed to keep out the rain, as could the U-shaped doorway, which was covered with a hide flap. Inside, people slept in willow-frame beds covered with furs. In the center a fire was kept burning with dried buffalo dung, or chips. The walls were adorned with paintings that depicted the men's triumphs in battle.

The tipi provided shelter for a large family. Household objects included tools, weapons, cooking utensils, buffalo robes, and backrests made of willow sticks tied with sinew. When the whole tribe came together in the summer, people arranged their tipis in a large circle. In hot weather the Arapaho raised the bottom edges of the covering to allow for a cool breeze. During the winter they often banked the tipi with a berm, or sloped earthen wall, for insulation against the cold. They also hung a buffalo hide "dew cloth" on the inside walls, from about shoulder height down to the damp ground. Decorated with paintings of battles, dreams, and visions, the dew cloth kept out moisture and provided a layer of insulating air. With a fire burning in the center of the earthen floor and buffalo robes lining the walls, tipis stayed warm during the coldest weather.

After the buffalo vanished from the land, the Arapaho no longer wandered the prairies. They had to abandon their tipis and settle in log cabins or plank houses on farms and ranches. Although now sheathed with canvas, modern tipis at powwows, Sun Dances, and other gatherings remain a powerful symbol of the independent spirit of the Arapaho.

Horses

At one time, the Arapaho had only sturdy dogs as working animals. They may have acquired their first horses as early as 1730, perhaps from the Comanche, who had traded or stolen the mounts from Spanish settlements in New Mexico. Horses quickly and completely transformed the Arapaho way of life. They rode these swift, powerful animals for traveling, hunting buffalo, trading, and waging war. They also used horses to carry heavy packs and pull travois. Mounted on their horses, the men could race after the thundering herds, killing large numbers of buffalo in a single hunt. They could

In the 1700s, the Arapaho acquired their first horses, which quickly became valuable in their independent way of life as hunters and warriors.

now readily supply themselves with enough meat to feed the band for months and an abundance of hides, bones, and other material for clothing, shelter, tools, and weapons. With horses the Arapaho could easily journey great distances, carrying their new wealth of goods and provisions. They came to prosper in large, comfortable camps, and they had more time to enjoy elaborate rituals.

To hunt buffalo, the Arapaho used strong, fast, well-trained horses with enough endurance to keep up with the stampeding herd. These buffalo horses were taught to courageously gallop alongside a stampeding bull so the rider could take point-blank aim with a bow and arrow. Yet a good horse had to have good instincts to jump clear of the buffalo's sharp horns. It had to be agile and alert, instantly responding to the rider's wishes. Holding a bow and arrow in his hands, the rider could guide the horse only by shifting his weight. The horse had to be sure-footed as it raced over the uneven ground. If it stumbled, the rider would be thrown under hundreds of pounding hooves.

Arapaho children's experience with horses began within days of their birth. When the band moved camp, mothers carried their babies on their backs as they rode along on their favorite horse. As soon as children were old enough to sit up, they rode on a travois or in the saddle with their mothers. When they were about five years old, children learned to ride alone on a gentle horse. Tied to the saddle, they were taught to hold the reins. At the age of seven or eight, children began to compete in horse races with each other. When they were about ten years old, boys started to care for the family horses, watering and pasturing them near camp.

Men occasionally caught wild mustangs from the many herds that now ranged throughout the American West. However, they preferred horses that had already been broken and trained. They usually procured these animals through barter with other native peoples or raids on enemy camps by small roving bands. A man who owned many horses was considered to be quite wealthy, and giving mounts away was highly respected among the Arapaho.

From an early age, the Arapaho became skilled riders relying on horses to carry people and belongings from one camp to another.

3. Lifeways

By singing and dancing at powwows, accompanied by drumming, the Arapaho continue to honor the cycle of life.

THE ARAPAHO BELIEVED THAT INDIVIDUALS ADVANCED THROUGH FOUR stages or "hills of life"—childhood, youth, adulthood, and old age. To acknowledge each phase of life, families and friends observed certain traditions and performed important rituals.

Cycle of Life

Birth. When a woman was about to give birth, she was assisted by a midwife and other older women. If needed, a man or woman who knew about herbs that eased childbirth might also be called in to help. As soon as a baby was born, family members prayed for its health and strength, and marked its face with red paint. The umbilical cord was dried and placed in a pouch decorated with beaded designs symbolizing good wishes for the baby. The pouch was tied to the cradleboard and later to the child's clothing so that the prayers of relatives would always accompany the young person.

A baby was placed in a U-shaped cradleboard made of a wood frame covered with buckskin. The cradleboard could be carried on the back, propped up by a tipi, or attached to a horse saddle. A mother would nurse her baby for as long as four years. She counted her child's age by "snows," marking a stick or her hide scraper with the passing of every winter.

Childhood. Ritual feasts were held to honor a child's growth and achievements. Between the ages of two and five, Arapaho children usually had their ears pierced in a ritual intended to help them overcome future pain and hardship. Aunts and uncles, as well as

Arapaho parents, like this proud young mother with her son, have always loved and cherished their children.

parents, were actively involved in the education and training of children. Children were encouraged to be well-mannered and respectful of adults, especially the elderly. They were expected to undertake chores promptly and respect the medicine bundles of the family and the traditions of the tribe. They were seldom punished and were taught primarily by example. Daughters learned how to perform household tasks and other duties by observing their mothers, aunts, and grandmothers. Young girls picked berries and did light work. As they grew older they began to dig roots, carry firewood, and undertake harder tasks, such as drying meat, cooking meals, dressing hides, sewing clothing, and making tipis. They also learned the art of decorating garments and other objects with porcupine quills, glass beads, and painted designs.

Boys learned the skills of hunting and warfare from their fathers and uncles. They made small bows and arrows to shoot rabbits and birds. Boys competed in rugged games and sports to develop strength and prove their courage. When they were in their early teens and had demonstrated their skill with weapons, they were asked to participate in their first buffalo hunt. If they proved themselves in this hunt, they might soon be allowed to go on their first raid.

Coming-of-Age. Unlike other Plains tribes, when they reached puberty, Arapaho girls and boys did not undergo a vision quest or other formal rite of passage. When she had her first period, a girl simply went into seclusion in a special menstrual lodge set aside for the women. When a young man killed his first buffalo, a feast was

Women not only taught practical skills to their daughters, they also instructed them in the traditions of the Arapaho people.

held in his honor. In a gesture of respect and compassion the youth was expected to give the buffalo to an old man who could no longer provide for himself. Both young women and men learned the importance of "giving back" to their family and the band.

When young people had acquired the necessary skills to support themselves and their own family, they were considered ready for marriage.

Marriage. Young men and women were usually kept apart before they were married, so marriages were usually arranged by parents or the man's female relatives. A woman could object to an arranged marriage, although she seldom did so, because the refusal would offend her parents. Couples sometimes eloped, returning to the camp in a few days. The groom then offered gifts to the bride's family, and his family would receive gifts in turn. However, marriage was usually revered as an important ceremony. On the wedding day there was an equal exchange of gifts, including horses, between the families of the bride and groom. The bride's family then set up a tipi and hosted a great feast, at which the couple was allowed to sit together for the first time.

If a man and woman did not get along, they could divorce each other. If a woman remarried soon after a divorce, her new husband might make a payment to the first husband.

Death. The Arapaho believed that often a person had a premonition four days before dying, which allowed for final arrangements and burial preparation. Upon death, the deceased was adorned in his or her finest clothes. The face and hair were painted red to help the departed's passage to the spirit world above. The body lay in state before being carried by horse to a burial site on a nearby hill. Cherished belongings were buried with the person, and a favorite horse was often killed and left at the grave. Any remaining property was given away to relatives, especially brothers and sisters. Stones were placed on the grave to prevent scavengers from digging up the body. They might also make a pile of stones as a monument to the battles, fasts, and other hardships in the departed's life. The Arapaho believed that the dead person's spirit remained for four days, so they brought food to the grave for several days. The personal medicine bundle of the deceased was taken away and buried by a medicine man if the spiritual power and knowledge of the bundle had not been handed down to another prior to the owner's death. Mourners cut their hair, wore old clothes, and made small cuts on their arms and legs to express their grief and suffering. After one year family and friends painted their faces and hair red to mark the end of their time of mourning.

Warfare

Arapaho men ranked among the best fighters and raiders on the Great Plains, and they were often raiding or waging war—against rival tribes, European traders, and finally United States soldiers. Their principal weapons included bows made of cedar and often backed with sinew, and arrows tipped with stone points. They also wielded stone war clubs and protected themselves with buffalo-hide shields. When going into battle or embarking on a raid, warriors painted their faces and called upon spiritual powers known as war medicine to bring them good fortune. Warriors were honored for stealing a horse or taking a scalp. Counting coup, or touching an enemy with a hand or stick, was especially esteemed—much more so than killing an enemy from a distance. Warriors were also admired for seizing a gun or other weapon from the hands of an enemy.

Hostilities often took the form of raids by small groups of men. Each raiding party hastily came together and broke up as soon as the warriors arrived home. Killing and scalping of enemies was not as important as seizing horses. Young men needed horses if they were going to marry and establish their own households. Risking their lives in these surprise attacks helped young men become more skillful as warriors. An experienced warrior led the raiding party. Usually in his thirties, he was joined by young men in their teens or early twenties. His proven ability inspired confidence that the party would capture many horses and return home safely. No one was forced to join a raiding party.

The Arapaho also went to war against other tribes on the Great Plains. When they first encountered the Cheyenne in the Black Hills, they immediately considered this tribe to be an enemy and tried to annihilate them. However, they soon sensed a kinship with these people who like themselves were relatively new to the Plains. Although they had to use signs to make themselves understood, the tribes both spoke Algonquian languages. Thereafter, the two tribes became good friends, and the alliance proved to be of mutual benefit.

To protect their hunting territory, the Arapaho battled several other tribes. Well-outfitted with horses and weapons acquired through trade or raids, they fought against the Crow north of the Platte River and against the Shoshone in the mountains farther west. After migrating south, they came into greater contact with Ute warriors, with whom they were frequently at war. The Arapaho readily defeated them on the open plains because the Ute were accustomed to the mountains and not skilled in fighting on horseback. However, in conflicts in the mountains the Ute had a clear advantage. To the east, the Arapaho had to deal with the Pawnee, who proved to be a

From an early age, boys learned to become skillful warriors with bows and arrows, war clubs, and long spears, as shown in this painting by Arapaho artist Carl Sweezy.

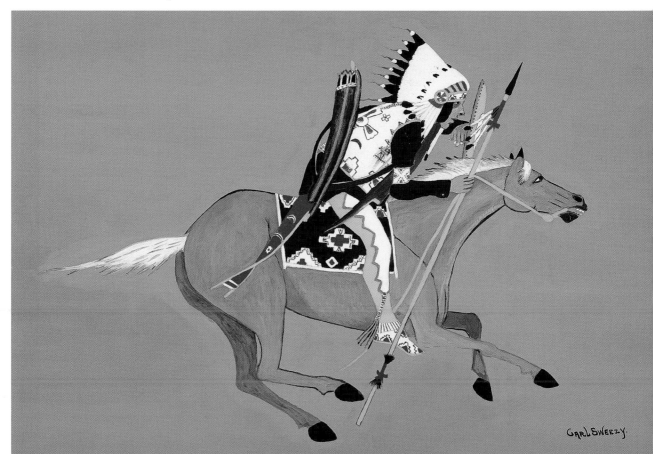

formidable enemy. However, to the south, at least until 1825, they enjoyed relatively peaceful relations with the Comanche and Kiowa, who had gradually moved north of the Platte River.

Often moving in their western territory, the Arapaho at first seldom encountered European trappers and traders who were making their way across the Plains and the mountains. However, they increasingly came into contact with them—to trade or make war. They apparently either directly traded with the Spanish or knew of their settlements in the Southwest, since they obtained items that had come from them. Over time they also began to trade with French and English traders and trappers who had ventured into their territory. They also fought against these newcomers. The Arapaho occasionally came into conflict with American trappers as well, although they also came to trade fairs to exchange horses for manufactured goods.

Over time this cycle of trade and conflict pressured the Arapaho into shifting alliances with other tribes. While living on the headwaters of the Cheyenne River in western South Dakota, near the Kiowa, they actively traded horses with tribes living on the Missouri River. However, by 1806 the Arapaho and Cheyenne had allied against the Sioux, who were pushing westward from the Missouri River. After moving farther west between the Yellowstone and Platte Rivers in what is now Wyoming, the Arapaho and some of the Cheyenne shifted alliances to the Sioux. About 1826 they started to drive the Kiowa and Comanche southward in order to take over the territory between the Platte and Arkansas Rivers. From the 1820s to 1840 conflicts raged with the Ute, Crow, and

Pawnee, but peace was established with the Kiowa and Comanche after these tribes had moved south of the Arkansas River.

Between 1834 and 1839 the United States established several trading posts in Arapaho territory—Bent's Fort on the Arkansas, Fort William on the North Platte, and Fort St. Vrain on the South Platte. Many Cheyenne had already moved into the region, and these forts now attracted the rest of the Cheyenne, who wished to trade there. The Arapaho's territory gradually shrank. By the 1840s the Sioux had come to dominate the territory around the North Platte River, where they competed with the Arapaho and Cheyenne for buffalo and other game. By 1850 the Arapaho were able to claim only what is known as the parks area at the foot of the Rocky Mountains. They were forced into a tense alliance with both the Sioux and the Cheyenne.

These conflicts with other tribes, including former allies, were intensified by the westward expansion of settlers and migrants passing through Arapaho territory on the Oregon and Santa Fe Trails. With the decline of the buffalo the tribes had to compete for the remaining animals. To find the herds, the Arapaho had to travel farther, so they needed more horses. Therefore, they increased their raids along the Santa Fe Trail and into New Mexico. These raids brought them into greater conflict with the United States. Yet they also became more dependent on trade goods, especially guns for hunting buffalo and fighting against rival tribes.

The Arapaho eventually united with many other Plains tribes and fought a losing war against U.S. soldiers.

Hunting and Gathering

On the Great Plains, food was generally abundant throughout the year. However, during winter blizzards and summer droughts people might go hungry or even starve to death. To ensure their survival, the Arapaho hunted and gathered cooperatively in bands. Generous with each other and with visitors, they believed that "Where there is true hospitality, not many words are needed."

Women picked wild fruits, nuts, and berries—especially chokecherries, wild plums, and silver buffalo berries. These ripe juicy fruits and berries were eaten fresh, cooked in soups and stews, or dried for the winter. Using a digging stick or buffalo scraper, they unearthed wild potatoes, prairie turnips, and other roots out on the plains. Prairie turnips were eaten raw, roasted or boiled, or dried for the winter. The most common meal was a stew made of meat and roots, especially wild potatoes and prairie turnips. People also enjoyed a kind of tea made with wild herbs. Grateful for what they were given, they often said, "Before eating, always take a little time to thank the food."

Arapaho men frequently hunted deer, elk, antelope, and small game. However, they lived primarily on buffalo, which provided food, clothing, and many other necessities. Like other tribes on the Great Plains, the Arapaho hunted buffalo in various ways. During the winter small groups of hunters occasionally strapped on snowshoes and stalked the buffalo, but most often bands went on large group hunts in the summer and fall. When they first moved onto the Plains, men, women, and children sometimes helped to stampede a

The Arapaho ate the meat of the buffalo, using the hides, bones, and horns for shelter, weapons, and tools.

herd over a cliff or into a buffalo trap, where hunters waited with bows and arrows. However, after they became skilled with horses, the Arapaho loved to race after the herds. Because reloading a gun was slow and cumbersome while on horseback, hunters usually speared or shot the buffalo with bows and arrows.

After the hunt, buffalo lay scattered over the plains. The men carefully skinned and butchered each animal. Very little of the carcass was ever wasted. The meat, fresh hide, and even the bones were thrown over the back of a horse and taken back to camp. People often ate the choice portions raw, especially the liver, kidney, and marrow from the leg bones. Fresh buffalo meat was boiled in soups and stews, or roasted. People savored the tongue, which was boiled in pots, and ribs, which were roasted over hot coals on wooden spits. However, most of the meat was preserved for later use. Women sliced the meat into thin strips, which were hung on racks to dry. Stored in leather pouches called *parfleches* (par-FLESH-es), the dried meat helped sustain the Arapaho during the winter and other times when food was scarce. Dried meat was also pounded into small pieces and mixed with fat and chokecherries to make pemmican. Stuffed into leather bags, pemmican was a highly nutritious food, favored by warriors on long journeys.

Although the following recipe includes some contemporary ingredients, it is reminiscent of meals traditionally prepared by the Arapaho.

Buffalo Meat Loaf

Ingredients

2 pounds ground buffalo meat
1 cup fine dry bread crumbs
3 eggs, lightly beaten
1 cup mushroom soup or milk
$1/3$ cup ketchup
6 ounces sliced mushrooms, fresh or canned
$1/2$ cup minced onion
1 teaspoon butter
1 teaspoon salt
$1/4$ teaspoon pepper
$1/2$ teaspoon thyme
$1/2$ cup minced parsley

Directions

Sauté mushrooms and onion in butter until onion is transparent. Combine with bread crumbs, thyme, and parsley. Lightly mix in buffalo meat, eggs, salt, pepper, and mushroom soup or milk. Place the mixture in a loaf pan. Spread ketchup evenly on top. Bake at 375 degrees for about 1 hour and 15 minutes. Let stand 10 to 15 minutes before slicing and serving.

Clothing and Jewelry

Women labored hard to make animal skins into clothing for their families. First, they scraped the flesh from deer, elk, and buffalo hides. Then, they stretched these skins on pegs to dry into stiff rawhide. The women next tanned the rawhide into soft buckskin, which they cut into pieces and sewed with sinew thread to make clothing. They decorated the clothing—as well as tipis and other items—with porcupine-quill embroidery and paintings. Designs often depicted spiritual beings or celestial bodies and included geometric patterns, such as elaborate diamonds or triangles.

In the early days, when they still lived in the north woods, Arapaho women wore a simple buckskin skirt, which overlapped on the right side, and a poncho-style shirt. In later years they wore a style of dress made of two deer or elk skins sewn together. Even later these dresses consisted of three skins, each of which had a wide, folded-down mantle known as a yoke. As they moved westward the Arapaho gradually came to adopt the styles of the Great Plains tribes. Women wore ankle-length dresses fringed with buckskin. Dresses were elaborately adorned with bands of quillwork or rows of elk teeth. They added knee-length leggings that were laced in the front and often decorated with yellow ochre and bands of quillwork.

Men wore a breechcloth, or breechclout, which was simply a rectangular piece of buckskin drawn between the legs and tied around the waist. They occasionally wore hip-length leggings, with bands of quillwork and long fringes on the sides. Sometimes they wore fringed poncho-style shirts made of buckskin. These shirts had an opening

*T*his Southern Arapaho woman posed for this photograph in moccasins and a buckskin dress adorned with shells.

*D*ressed in cloth garments, but with traditional moccasins and long hair, these Southern Arapaho men posed in front of a log cabin.

so they could be pulled over the head and tied with thongs at the waist. Both women and men wore moccasins made of rawhide soles and buckskin tops.

Arapaho clothing was often adorned with bold, colorful paintings and elaborate quillwork. Designs tended to be simpler than those of other Plains tribes, perhaps because the Arapaho continued to use quillwork long after the other tribes had adopted beading. Popular designs included stripes, scallops, diamonds, and arrows. During the winter people kept warm in buffalo-skin robes draped over their shoulders and tied in the front with thongs. The tanned side of the robe was often adorned with painted designs or intricate quillwork. They also trudged through the snow in snowshoes made from wooden frames laced with strips of rawhide.

Hairstyles changed over time. Women once wore their hair loose, but later adopted the style of parting and braiding their hair on both sides. The braids fell over the shoulders in front. To appear fierce, warriors parted their long hair and left it hanging on either side of their face. Later they braided their hair or tied it back with a scalp lock. Originally, the Arapaho did not wear warbonnets, like the Sioux, Cheyenne, and other Plains tribes. Men simply tied a single feather or cluster of feathers to the hair at the crown of their heads. The feathers were often further ornamented with tufts of horsehair lightly dyed red or green. Men also wore rawhide hats with a visor, which shaded the eyes from the sun. Men also liked to wear leather armbands decorated with bands of quillwork. They carried fans made of eagle or hawk feathers and fringed purses adorned with quillwork. In the late nineteenth century men came to wear breast-plates made of hairpipe beads. Since their clothing had no pockets, both men and women carried personal belongings in pouches tied to leather belts or thongs on their clothing.

People wore earrings of shell, bone, or feathers. The Arapaho were sometimes referred to as the Big Bead or Blue Bead Indians because they came to favor large blue beads. These may have been made of turquoise obtained through trade in the Southwest. Warriors often wore necklaces with symbolic designs based on their dreams. The Arapaho also adorned themselves with tattoos by pricking the skin with cactus needles and rubbing charcoal into the cuts. Men

The Arapaho often adorned themselves with beautiful necklaces made of beads, shells, bones, or animal teeth.

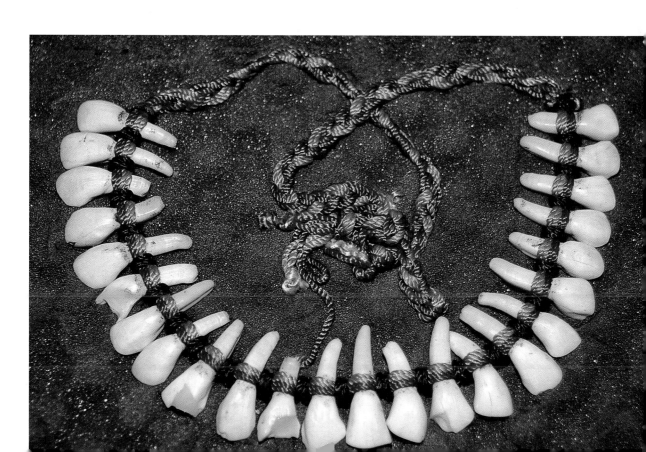

often favored three small circles across their chests, while women typically had a small circle on their foreheads. Young women painted streaks on their cheeks, forehead, and nose.

People wore special regalia for warfare and ceremonies. Warriors equipped themselves with shields of tough buffalo hide. These shields were covered with buckskin and were often painted with the image of a turtle. They also wore otter skins because it was believed that these animals could protect warriors in battle. For each of the four days of the Sun Dance, participants donned certain articles of dress. Similarly, members of the societies added distinctive touches to their clothing that indicated their social position. People also painted their faces and bodies, especially for ceremonies. In the Sun Dance the face, chest, and arms were painted. Women painted streaks down their faces in times of war. Old women painted a red spot on each cheek to symbolize peace, a spot on the forehead and one between the eyes to signify a buffalo calf, and a line from the mouth to the chin to symbolize a road. Paint on the face usually signified happiness. Both men and women painted the part in their hair with red ochre to symbolize "the path of the sun."

Over time, the Arapaho adopted the warbonnet, warshirts, and beading techniques and styles of other Plains tribes. When the buffalo herds vanished, people had to switch from buffalo robes to blankets. However, the blankets were as finely beaded as the buffalo robes had been quilled. They continued to embrace a spiritual approach to the decoration of clothing. Long dresses, in particular, featured elaborate beadwork. Pressured by missionaries while living on the reservation, the Arapaho gradually adopted European styles of dress. Yet today many people continue to sew and adorn clothing in the traditional ways of their mothers and grandmothers.

Handicrafts

The Arapaho crafted many everyday objects, ranging from stones for grinding seeds to fine porcupine quill ornaments. They carved wooden bowls, some of which had artistic and religious significance. They also made shallow baskets from plant fibers and pipes from black stone. Women were renowned for their finely dressed hides and the quality of their handiwork. They made tipi covers, clothing,

The Arapaho's strong sense of color and intricate design is reflected in modern powwow dress, notably the feathered bustles on men's regalia.

storage pouches, and many other objects, which they adorned with quills, beads, or painted designs that symbolized religious beliefs. Men painted tipis and other leather goods with designs showing battle events—although this work had to be supervised by The Seven Old Women, who were in charge of decoration and handiwork. Popular designs in painting, quilling, and beadwork known as "crossing paths" symbolized the connection between the four cardinal directions—north, south, east, and west.

People came to rely on the buffalo not only for their meat but for their hides, horns, hooves, and bones. For the Arapaho the buffalo provided the materials for most of their tools and household objects. They made good use of virtually every part of the buffalo in crafting over sixty kinds of objects, including tipis, clothing, household utensils, tools, and weapons. Leaving the shaggy hair on, women tanned buffalo robes for winter clothing. They also tanned the hairless skins into supple buckskin for tipi covers, clothing, and small pouches. Sinew was used as sewing thread and bowstrings. Men made tools—points for arrows and spears, knives, scrapers, and needles—from the bones. The Arapaho later traded for metal knives. Horns were softened and shaped into spoons, cups, and ladles. Strung on rawhide cords, the hooves were made into noisy rattles. Another kind of rattle, with pebbles inside, was made of rawhide stretched over a framework of wood fitted with a wooden handle. Buffalo hair could be woven into rope halters and bridles. The shaggy hair could also be used as padding for saddles and stuffing for balls, as well as ornaments for tipis, clothing, and war clubs. Even the tail could be used as a flyswatter.

They carried water in animal skins and cooked meat and vegetables in a pot made from the lining of a buffalo stomach. They even burned dried manure, or buffalo chips, as fuel for their fires.

Stiff, durable rawhide, in particular, was an especially versatile material. Rawhide was fashioned into belts and moccasin soles. It was stretched to cover drums and war shields. Most horse equipment, including bridles and saddles, was made of rawhide. Rawhide strips could be used as strings and straps for hobbling horses or lashing a travois. Rawhide could also be braided into tough ropes, but one of the most important uses was in making leather pouches known as parfleches. The Arapaho made parfleches in various sizes for storing food, clothing, and other personal belongings. Since they were often on the move, their household goods had to be light and durable, and parfleches were well suited for carrying them. To make a parfleche, a woman scraped a piece of rawhide until it looked like white parchment. Then it was folded and stitched together. Shaped like envelopes of varying sizes, these pouches were painted in rich colors with bold geometric designs. These patterns symbolized animals, everyday life, or wonders of the universe.

One of the oldest parfleche designs featured red triangles resembling bear claws or parts of bear feet. Green triangles may also have symbolized bear claws or possibly mountain peaks. Red blocks often represented riverbeds, especially those with red banks. Double lines forming a border around the outside of a parfleche may have symbolized the familiar paths of animals or people. These designs may also have depicted the camp circle, or even the entire world. One of

Women often adorned moccasins and clothing with designs made from porcupine quills and later with beads obtained through trade.

the most common paintings featured blue triangles as tents, blue lines around the outside as the tent pegs, and the squares in the corners as the ends of the earth. Other designs included eyes and the paths of the rotating sun and moon.

After the designs were painted on clothing or a pouch, the artist prayed, following which the handmade object could be used.

4. Beliefs

Deeply religious, the Arapaho have revered the wide, open plains of their ancestral homeland for many generations.

WHEN WE SHOW OUR RESPECT FOR OTHER LIVING THINGS, THEY RESPOND with respect for us.

—Arapaho saying

Religious beliefs centered on the Creator, Manito or Man-Above, who made the world and the Arapaho people. By praying and offering gifts to the Creator, the intensely religious Arapaho believed that they would enjoy good health and happiness. They believed in the life-giving rays of the sun, to which they prayed so much that early explorers thought they might be sun worshippers. The Arapaho also viewed themselves as part of nature, believing "All plants are our brothers and sisters. They talk to us, and if we listen, we can hear them."

Medicine bundles were central to Arapaho beliefs. These bundles held sacred objects that were believed to have great powers and to be selected for the individual by the Creator. The objects to be placed in their medicine bundles were revealed to individuals in dreams and vision quests. During times of sickness or war a person invoked the power of the medicine bundle in appealing to the Creator. Religious leaders known as medicine men, or shamans, also had their own medicine bundles for ceremonies.

The Arapaho believed that people became sick when they did not show proper respect for the Creator. They believed that simply thinking of illness or death might bring it upon themselves. When a person became ill, relatives opened their medicine bundles and

*T*he Arapaho frequently prayed to the sun, which they regarded as the source
of all life on earth.

prayed to the Creator. They would sometimes offer gifts of food or
property in hopes of making their loved one better. In serious cases
they called upon the medicine man. Medicine men attempted to cure
illnesses by having the patient sweat in a lodge and by wafting the
smoke of roots, twigs, and herbs over the patient.

Other medicine bundles belonged to the lodges or the whole band. Carefully wrapped in an ornately decorated bundle, the flat pipe was the most sacred object of the tribe. This three-foot-long pipe was kept by seven respected elders of the tribe. The pipe, which represented the power of the Creator on earth, was unwrapped and smoked only on the most sacred occasions. When the tribe moved, the lead rider carried the flat pipe.

Rites and Ceremonies

In the eighteenth century, perhaps as late as 1800, the Sun Dance, also known as the Medicine Lodge or the Offerings Lodge ceremony, became the most important Arapaho ceremony. After a long winter in scattered bands they came together on the plains in June or July. The ceremony revolved around the Offerings Lodge. In this ritual a center pole and brush shelter became a sacred place on the windswept plains.

At the heart of the lodge was the Sacred Wheel, which was placed on an altar. The parts of the Sacred Wheel symbolized the celestial bodies and the weather. The disk at the center represented the sun, and the band painted around it symbolized the water. Markings on the sides represented the Four Old Men who controlled the winds. Beads and feathers symbolized the sky and rain.

Although the Sun Dance was a test of endurance and sacrifice, unlike other Plains tribes the Arapaho did not practice extreme self-torture in this yearly event. They concentrated on renewing themselves and making sacrificial offerings to the Creator.

Today the Northern Arapaho continue to actively participate in the Sun Dance. Many Southern Arapaho make an annual pilgrimage to the Wind River Reservation and join them in this celebration.

Games

People enjoyed many games of skill and strength, and they frequently held athletic competitions, such as races on foot or horseback. Games were also an integral part of the Sun Dance and other ceremonies. One of the Arapaho's favorite contests of skill was the hoop-and-dart game, also called hoop-and-pole game, which was played by many Native American tribes. The hoop was made from a supple green branch, preferably willow, which was bent into a circle and tied with rawhide. Plant fiber or sinew was then interwoven into the hoop to form a web, or net, of squares, rectangles, and triangles. The hoop could be placed on the ground, hung from a tree, or most often rolled along the ground as contestants took turns throwing their darts at it. The score depended on how close to the center a dart or pole had struck. This game ended when one of the players acquired a predetermined number of points.

Popular with many tribes across North America, the hand game called *gaqutit* was a favorite Arapaho pastime. Each tribe had its own rules, but the object remained the same—to guess which hand held a hidden button. Each team had a button: one painted red and the other black. The leader shifted the button from one hand to the other, or slipped it behind his back to a teammate. To conceal the button, they could pass one hand over another or hide their hands behind their back. The opponents carefully studied their hands, facial expressions, and body language as they tried to keep track of the button. When a member of the opposing team felt he knew the location of the button, he pointed his thumb to the hand and cried out. If he guessed correctly, his team would be awarded tally sticks and then conceal the button. However, if he guessed wrong, his team had to relinquish a number of tally sticks and the other team again hid the button.

While the game was being played, all the team members sang and danced in a jerky manner to confuse their opponents, yet their hands and arms moved in perfect rhythm to the song. A contest lasted a long time, often into the early hours of the morning. The game was sometimes played between members of tribes speaking different languages, but this was not a problem, since the game relied primarily on gestures, not spoken words. Like other Plains tribes, the Arapaho most often played this game in the winter. Both men and women played the hand game, but never with each other. As many as twenty or even thirty people would gather in a tipi, the two sides facing each other across the fire. People usually played in good spirits, clapping their hands and beating the ground if they guessed right.

Storytelling

The Arapaho did not have a written language. If they wished to record a historic event, they sometimes drew pictures on buckskin. However, they relied most heavily on the art of the spoken word. Storytellers both amused children and instructed people in their history. Young children were encouraged from an early age to describe and remember people and events in vivid detail. Storytelling continues to be a favorite Arapaho pastime to this very day. Children like to gather around parents and grandparents to listen to stories, through which the young of each generation still learn about the beliefs and customs of their people.

The Arapaho enjoyed stories including those that explained how they had come to prosper as buffalo hunters and warriors.

Here is a story about how the Arapaho learned to provide for themselves:

How the Arapaho Came to Prosper

Long ago, a man began to wonder how the Arapaho might hunt the great herds of buffalo. Devoting a great deal of thought to this question, he went away and fasted for several days. He did so many times until a dream came to him, and a voice spoke to him.

He went back to his people and made a large corral with tree limbs stuck in the ground as fence posts and with willow branches woven around them. One side of the corral had no fence—it opened to a cliff with rocks at the bottom.

Four runners with great speed and stamina were then sent out to the herd, approaching windward so that the buffalo would not catch their scent. With two of the runners on each side, they drove the buffalo into the enclosure. The buffalo were stampeded, raising a cloud of dust. Unable to see, the buffalo plunged over the cliff and were killed on the rocks below.

After a while, the man decided that he should also provide horses for the Arapaho. As the people followed the buffalo they had only small dogs to drag their belongings, and women had to carry part of the load on their backs. However, there were now many wild horses on the Great Plains.

So the man built another large corral, leaving a wide opening. Wild horses were driven into the corral, and the gate was quickly closed. Men ran the horses around the corral until they became very tired and could be lassoed. It took a long time to break the horses, and in the beginning, there was just one horse for each family. However, this was not enough, and more wild mustangs were caught and broken. After a few years people bred their horses, and every man soon had his own herd.

The man then made the first bow and four arrows, which he tipped with sharp points honed from the short rib of a buffalo. Going off alone, he waited, hidden in the trees, near a buffalo path. He shot the first buffalo that came down the trail, then he killed three more.

Returning to his people, he said, "Bring the pack horses. There are four buffalo in the timber, and plenty of meat."

The people were now able to get meat, without driving the buffalo into corrals. They also learned to pursue buffalo on horses. They could now easily hunt buffalo, and they had more meat. But they had nothing with which to cut up the meat. So the man showed the people how to make sharp knives—from pieces of flint and the shoulder blades of buffalo.

The people needed to cook the meat, so the man showed them how to make a fire with a piece of flint and a little tinder. Using soft, dry wood as tinder, he struck a spark with the flint, and the tinder soon glowed orange. He put grass and then twigs on the small flame, which grew into a campfire on which people could now cook their buffalo meat.

Because of these new ways of hunting and providing for themselves, the Arapaho came to prosper as they moved onto the sprawling prairies.

5. Changing World

Over the years the Arapaho have had to face many new difficulties.

EARLY TRADERS FOUND THAT THE ARAPAHO WERE QUITE FRIENDLY, AND EAGER to exchange goods. The Arapaho often visited the Mandan villages along the Knife River in present-day North Dakota. They also served as middlemen in trade between the northern and southern tribes of Plains Indians. For some time, the Arapaho traded with other tribes for knives, guns, and other items of European manufacture without often meeting any Europeans. They may have encountered European traders as early as the 1730s. By the early nineteenth century they were actively trading buffalo robes and animal skins to Mexicans and Americans for metal tools and weapons. However, the traders also brought alcohol and introduced diseases against which the Arapaho had little resistance.

Native peoples, including the Arapaho, sometimes also fought with the traders and trappers who encroached on their territory. Nonetheless, the fur trade gradually flourished and was a lucrative business by the turn of the nineteenth century. Powerful chiefs, such as Bear Tooth, continued to openly welcome the newcomers and managed to keep peace into the early 1800s. However, in 1837 a major war broke out between the Southern Arapaho and Southern Cheyenne against the Comanche. Peace was restored by 1840, but the opening of the Oregon Trail only led to an increase in westward migration and more conflicts. Settlers not only trespassed on native lands but often treated Plains Indians with ignorance and hate.

The Arapaho played a major role in the ensuing wars for the Great Plains. The Northern Arapaho allied with the Sioux and

Northern Cheyenne, while the Southern Arapaho ended up siding with the Southern Cheyenne, Comanche, and Kiowa. On September 8, 1851, representatives of eleven Plains tribes, including the Arapaho, met with U.S. government officials in what came to be known as the Horse Creek Council. David D. Mitchell, the superintendent of Indian Affairs, addressed the assembled chiefs, outlining the wishes and demands of the federal government. He wanted assurance that settlers would be able to journey across the Plains without threat of attack, warning that forts would be built to protect them. He explained that they would be compensated for the destruction of the buffalo and the grass eaten by ranchers' cattle. He told them that they would have their own tribal lands. Subsequently, the Arapaho and Cheyenne were granted territory between the Platte and Arkansas Rivers.

Hoping for lasting peace, the Arapaho and Cheyenne agreed to the Fort Laramie Treaty in which they surrendered most of their territory in exchange for these lands and an annuity of $50,000 in goods for fifty years (later reduced to $15,000 without the knowledge and consent of the tribes). The Arapaho also retained open fishing and hunting rights, but serious problems ensued. As wagon trains rolled through Arapaho territory, settlers hunted game and sometimes attacked Arapaho bands. Pushed westward by American pioneers, other tribes also began to hunt in the dwindling lands of the Arapaho. Gold miners also poured into their territory around 1858, setting up camps and towns in violation of the treaty and without any regard for the Arapaho.

In 1859, under terms of the Fort Wise Treaty, the Arapaho and Cheyenne agreed to live in a specific region while keeping hunting rights throughout their territory. In February 1861 the Southern Arapaho agreed to another treaty with the U.S. government in which they surrendered all of their land except a small reservation in eastern Colorado. However, despite the continuing loss of land, conflicts with settlers and soldiers persisted. When retaliating for native attacks against settlers who were trespassing on their land, army troops often did not

In negotiations with military officials, the Arapaho had to lay down their arms and abandon their traditional way of life.

distinguish between one native band and another. In 1864 hundreds of Arapaho and Cheyenne were camped peacefully near Sand Creek in Colorado, which the U.S. Army had declared to be a safe place for them. However, they were ambushed as they slept by U.S. troops under Colonel John M. Chivington, as part of a campaign to drive all native peoples from Colorado. At least 130 people, including many women and children, were slaughtered in what came to be known as the Sand Creek Massacre.

In retaliation the Southern Arapaho, led by Little Raven, united with the Cheyenne in unrelenting attacks against settlers and soldiers for six months. The cycle of violence escalated into the so-called Indian Wars of 1865–1868. However, the Plains tribes had lost many people to warfare, disease, and starvation. Cut off from the buffalo herds, the Arapaho and Cheyenne reluctantly took part in the Medicine Lodge Council of 1867 on the Medicine Lodge River in Kansas. Little Raven, a talented orator and diplomat, as well as chief of the tribe, represented the tribes in these negotiations. In the ensuing Medicine Lodge Treaty, Southern Arapaho and Southern Cheyenne agreed to cede all their territory north of the Arkansas River and move to a reservation in Indian Territory in what is now Oklahoma. The treaty granted the Southern Arapaho and Southern Cheyenne a tract of land in the Cherokee Outlet in Oklahoma, near the Kansas state line and the Osage reservation. However, the tribes mistakenly settled on a different parcel of land. Citing the poor soil and the lack of woodlands and water, they asked for another location. By

*H*ere, *Little Raven posed with his young daughter, two sons, and Colonel William Bent at Fort Dodge, Kansas, in 1869.*

proclamation of President Ulysses S. Grant in August 1869, they were given a new reservation along the North Canadian and Washita Rivers. Reservation leaders worked hard to establish cattle herds, hay fields, and large gardens to sustain their people.

Meanwhile, the Northern Arapaho resisted any attempts to take away their lands. Living in the Powder River country of Wyoming, they occasionally skirmished with settlers and soldiers. By terms of the Fort Laramie Treaty of 1868, they were supposed to settle with the Sioux on the Pine River Reservation in South Dakota Territory. However, holding out for their own reservation, the Northern Arapaho stayed in Wyoming. They also refused to join the Southern Arapaho in Indian Territory.

Along with the Sioux, Northern Cheyenne, and other tribes, Northern Arapaho warriors swept down on General George Custer and his troops at the Battle of the Little Bighorn on June 25, 1876. The soldiers were quickly annihilated in the battle, and the tribes celebrated their great victory as they went their separate ways. However, after the defeat at Little Big Horn, the U.S. Army launched a winter campaign in the Powder River country, in which they attacked and destroyed native villages. The Arapaho surrendered at Camp Robinson, where they remained for a year as virtual prisoners of war.

Although traditionally enemies, the Shoshone recognized the plight of the Northern Arapaho and invited them to settle on their 2.3-million-acre reservation in Wyoming in 1878. The U.S. government accepted the arrangement, which the Shoshone considered temporary refuge for the Arapaho. However, the arrangement became permanent.

In 1927 the Shoshone appealed to the Court of Claims and were paid for the value of the half of the land that they had given to Arapaho. Although the two tribes were no longer foes, they continued to live in separate communities on the reservation. In 1937 the name was formally changed to the Wind River Reservation. People struggled to sustain themselves on government aid until 1947, when tribal leaders gained control of the mineral resources on their land. Thereafter, 15 percent of the income from mineral royalties went to community services and the remaining 85 percent was distributed to tribal members in monthly payments.

In 1890 the Southern Arapaho actively began to spread the word of the Ghost Dance religion that was sweeping through many of the Plains tribes. A Southern Arapaho named Sitting Bull had lived among the Northern Arapaho and returned to the reservation in Indian Territory. He spoke widely of a desperately hopeful vision—the settlers would be covered over, and the plains would return to a natural state. The buffalo would then return to the plains, and native people would again be able to live a traditional way of life. During the height of the Ghost Dance, in 1891, the United States government began the process of allotting, or dividing, Arapaho and Cheyenne reservation lands in Oklahoma among individual tribe members, each receiving 160 acres. The remainder of the 4-million-acre reservation was opened up to settlers. On April 19, 1892, nonnatives were allowed to purchase some of these lands, but they still trespassed on Arapaho farms and ranches. They also stole livestock, equipment, wood, and other

*E*ven after they were forced onto reservations, the Arapaho had to surrender more of their tribal lands.

property. Demands for tribal lands continued, and in 1902 and 1906, the U.S. Congress passed laws that encouraged the sale of allotted Indian lands. Impoverished Arapaho and Cheyenne people were forced to sell their lands, and eventually only about 75,000 of the nearly half-million acres remained in the reservation.

When placed on the reservations, the Arapaho faced considerable pressure to abandon their customs and traditional religious beliefs and adopt Euro-American culture. Missionaries tried to convert people to Christianity, and Arapaho children were taken from their families and sent away to boarding schools. As part of a "civilization program," a school opened in 1870 on the Oklahoma reservation and continued as a boarding school until 1908, when it was combined with the Southern Cheyenne school.

With the passage of the Oklahoma Indian Welfare Act of 1937, the Arapaho and Cheyenne Nations were able to reorganize their governments under their own constitution and bylaws. The southern tribes established the Cheyenne-Arapaho Business Committee, which consists of seven members from each tribe. Committee members are elected to two-year terms by popular vote, with headquarters in Concho, Oklahoma. The Northern Arapaho formed the Arapaho Business Council with headquarters in Fort Washakie, Wyoming.

Arapaho Language

The Arapaho speak one of the Algonquian languages, most of which belong to the northeastern United States, eastern Canada, and the Great Lakes region. Yet there are seven Algonquian languages spoken on the Plains, including Cheyenne, Blackfoot, and Gros Ventre, as well as Arapaho. Today there are only a few speakers of the Arapaho language, and the Northern Arapaho have established programs in reservation schools to keep the language alive. The following samples are drawn from a revised Internet version of an original English-Arapaho dictionary produced in 1983 by Zdenek Salzmann and the Arapaho Language and Culture Commission (ALCC) for the Northern Arapaho tribe on the Wind River Indian Reservation, in Wyoming.

Arapaho language is complex, but the following key and examples should be helpful for basic pronunciation of words.

Here are the letters: b c e h i k n o s 3 t u w x y '

The last of these symbols (') is the glottal stop, a catch in the throat, as at the beginning of each of the two syllables in the English expression "uh oh!" This is indicated by a '. It is made by momentarily closing the throat, as in the Arapaho word *ho'* for "dirt."

e   as in b*e*t
i   as in b*i*t
o   as in g*o*t
u   as in p*u*t

Long vowels are indicated by the doubling or tripling of the same vowel sounds above or by combinations (diphthongs) of different vowel sounds.

ee   is close in sound to the English short "a" sound, as in b*a*t.

ii   is similar to the long "e" in English, such as in b*ee*t.

oo   is much like the vowel sound in c*au*ght or f*ou*ght.

uu   is a long "u" sound as in the English word d*u*de.

Diphthongs are combinations of the short vowel sounds, for example:

ei   as in w*ei*ght.

ou   as in b*oa*t.

Triple vowels are extra long vowels or diphthongs that are held even longer and usually have a stress at the beginning and end. For example, the word booo is a long "oo" sound with an added and stressed "o" sound on the end. Usually the stress is on the first vowel and the last.

eee   is an extra long "e" or three "e"s put together.

iii   is an extra long "i" or three "i"s put together.

ooo   is an extra long "o", or three "o"s put together.

uuu   is an extra long "u" or three "u"s put together.

eii   is an "ei" sound with an "i" sound added to the end.

oee   is an "oe" sound held somewhat longer.

ouu   is an "ou" sound with a "u" added to the end.

Consonants are generally pronounced as in English, with the following exceptions:

b   is slightly less pronounced than the English "b" at the beginning and in the middle of words, and sounds like a "p" at the end.

c   is between an English "j" and "ch." It is more like a "j" at the beginning of words.

h   is like the English "h," but when at the end of a word or syllable, it is breathed (air is forced out slightly).

k   is a blend of "k" and "g," but more like "g" at the beginning of words, and more like "k" at the end.

s   is like the English "s" as in *sea*, but is never like a "z" sound as in *trees*.

t   sounds like an English "d," as in *dot*, at the beginning of words, but more like a "t" elsewhere.

3   is similar to the unvoiced "th" sound in English, as in *thin*, but never like the voiced "th" sound as in *the* or *that*.

w   is the same as "w" in *water*, but in Arapaho you must also make the "w" rounded-lip shape when it is at the end, as in the Arapaho word *woow*, meaning now.

x   does not have a similar sound in English, but is like the "ch" sound in German, as in *ich* or *machen*.

y   is the same as the English "y," but must be shaped with the mouth at the end of words, too.

Following are some everyday words used by the Arapaho.

arrow	who3
arrowhead	woosoo3
bear	wox
beaver	hebes
bird	nii'eihii
bow (for shooting arrows)	beete'
buffalo bull	heneecee
herd of buffalo	hii3einoon
buffalo	chipsbiihi3ii
buffalo cow	nonooni
buffalo hide	heecen
buffalo calf	nihoonou'u
buffalo robe	biixou, hii3einoonou
corn (ear of corn)	beskootee
coyote	koo'oh
creek	koh'owu'
day	hiisi'
deer	bih'ih
dog	he3

eagle, bald	heetesee'eit
elk	hiwoxuu
fire	sitee
food	bii3ib
horse	woxhoox, woxuuhoox
house	ho'oowu'
ice	wo'ow
moon	biikousiis
mountain	hohe'
night	tece'
people	hineniteeno'
prairie	hi3o'owuu'
rainbow	noyoot
river	niicii, niicie
snow	hiii
star	ho3o'
sun	hiisiis
tobacco	siisoowoo
tree	hohoot

6. New Ways

Today, many Arapaho in Wyoming live in small houses on the Wind River Reservation.

OVER THE PAST SEVERAL DECADES THE ARAPAHO HAVE BEEN ACTIVELY involved in many efforts to retain control over their land and resources in both Oklahoma and Wyoming. In 1883 President Chester A. Arthur issued an executive order to take 7,500 acres of the Cheyenne-Arapaho reservation in Oklahoma for military use. After military operations ended at Fort Reno, the property was to be returned to the tribes, as specified by the original agreement. However, the U.S. Department of Agriculture then took possession of the land, and tribal leaders have since been working to recover this portion of their reservation. These misdeeds by individuals, businesses, and governments have increasingly forced the Arapaho into federal court in a new version of the Indian Wars as they fight to defend their rights.

During the 1980s the Arapaho and Shoshone discovered that large amounts of oil on the Wind River Reservation were being stolen. Portions of their land were leased to various oil companies, but lack of government supervision allowed the companies to take advantage of the tribes. In 1989 the Arapaho successfully protested against a U.S. Forest Service plan to make a sacred site in Big Horn National Forest into a tourist attraction. During a 1990 drought the Northern Arapaho also decided to withhold water on the Wind River Reservation from ditches that irrigated adjoining lands. Farmers and ranchers, along with county officials, disputed the Arapaho's right to manage their own water. Although a Wyoming court upheld the tribe's position, the state supreme court issued a stay in 1991.

Today there are about 4,000 Northern Arapaho living on the Wind River Reservation. A six-member elected business council manages tribal operations and represents the tribe in issues with the federal government. The Northern Arapaho have no constitution and no bylaws, so the business council tries to operate by consensus, in the best interests of the community. A general council made up of all eligible voters on the reservation has veto rights over any of their actions. Since 1975 congressional legis-

A rapaho children attend both public and private schools, such as Saint Stephen's Indian School, on the Wind River Reservation.

lation has enabled the Arapaho to contract for grants and programs previously administered by federal agencies. The business council has since been able to directly manage funds for social programs on the reservation. The main economic activities are ranching and crafts, along with a few small businesses. Some people have jobs with the school district or tribal government. However, most families continue to depend on their monthly royalty payments, since there are few jobs available in the region and unemployment remains high (up to 80 percent).

With about 3,000 members the Southern Arapaho receive only a very small annual royalty payment from several oil wells on the reservation. Unemployment, however, can be as high as 70 percent. It is lower than on the Wind River Reservation because more jobs are available in nearby Oklahoma City and other urban areas. Having agreed to joint constitutional government since 1935, tribal members now elect four Arapaho and four Cheyenne to the business committee. The committee contracts with government agencies for several social programs and oversees tribal businesses, notably bingo, cigarette sales, and farming.

As they struggle for economic survival the Arapaho are also trying to preserve the traditions of their ancestors. Over the years most Northern and Southern Arapaho people have become Christians, and a Catholic mission established on the reservation in Wyoming serves many people. Some Arapaho became Mennonites, and others became members of the Native American Church. Many people, however, continue to practice their traditional religion centered around the Sun Dance Lodge. Yet this annual ritual of sacrifice and renewal, along with other sacred practices, was nearly lost among the Southern Arapaho when elders did not instruct successors. By World War II the Southern Arapaho were apprenticing themselves to religious leaders among the Northern Arapaho. These leaders are now found only in Wyoming, although many Southern Arapaho practice healing ceremonies.

Only a few people, mostly Southern Arapaho, continue to speak the language. However, a language program has been estab-

Many Arapaho people have embraced Christianity and attend churches, such as Saint Stephen's Indian Mission in Wyoming.

In fancy regalia, this young man carries on the traditions of the Arapaho as he dances at a Wind River powwow.

lished on the Wind River Reservation. In 2002 Southern Arapaho and Southern Cheyenne tribal leaders negotiated the purchase of the site of the Sand Creek Massacre in Colorado. The tribes have been working with Senator Ben Nighthorse Campbell (R-Colo.), the National Park Service, and other federal officials to preserve Sand Creek as a national historic site. Tribal leaders plan to work with the northern tribes and the National Park Service to establish a memorial to honor those who died at Sand Creek. A delegation of elders, chiefs, and other tribal members recently issued a proclamation and presented gifts to the key officials who were involved in acquiring Sand Creek.

Each year, the northern and southern branches of the tribes host powwows on the reservations, in which dancers and drummers recall the traditions of their ancestors. These events usually include giveaways, a popular custom of many Plains Indians, including the Arapaho. Families offer gifts in honor of a relative, to express gratitude, or to assume a new responsibility. The Arapaho are working together in these and many other ways, particularly in religious ceremonies, to ensure that the history and traditions of their people are passed along to future generations.

More about

the Arapaho

Timeline

mid-1500s The Spanish bring horses to the American Southwest.

before 1700 The Arapaho migrate from the Great Lakes region to the Great Plains and adopt a nomadic way of life.

about 1730 The Arapaho acquire their first horses.

1803 The United States acquires the Louisiana Purchase, an enormous tract of land that encompasses Arapaho territory.

1835 The tribe separates into two groups, the Northern Arapaho, who move near the North Platte River in Wyoming, and the Southern Arapaho, who live near the Arkansas River in Colorado.

1851 At the Horse Creek Council, U.S. government officials persuade the Arapaho to live within certain boundaries.

1864 Colorado soldiers massacre Southern Arapaho and Cheyenne men, women, and children in their camp at Sand Creek.

1867 The Southern Arapaho move onto an Oklahoma reservation with the Southern Cheyenne.

1874 U.S. Army troops and Shoshone warriors attack the Northern Arapaho, leaving the survivors without food and tipis for the winter.

1878 The Northern Arapaho settle with the Shoshone on the Wind River Reservation in Wyoming.

1887 The U.S. Congress passes the General Allotment Act, which requires the division of reservations, including Arapaho lands, into parcels owned by individuals.

1892 The Arapaho-Cheyenne reservation in Oklahoma is opened to non-native settlers.

1904 The Northern Arapaho and Shoshone lose two-thirds of their land when the Wind River Reservation is allotted, or divided, into individual plots.

1930 The last Offerings Lodge Ceremony is held in Oklahoma.

1930s Allotment is ended in the New Deal administration of President Franklin D. Roosevelt, and the Northern Arapaho regain some of their land.

1961 The Arapaho and Cheyenne win a multimillion-dollar settlement from the U.S. government.

1989 The Northern Arapaho successfully protest a U.S. Forest Service plan to turn a sacred site in Big Horn National Forest into a tourist attraction.

1990 The Northern Arapaho withhold water from irrigation ditches during a drought on the Wind River Reservation. The Wyoming state supreme court orders a stay a year later.

2002 Cheyenne and Arapaho tribal leaders negotiate the purchase of the site of the Sand Creek Massacre in Colorado, which will be preserved as a national historic landmark.

Notable People

Black Bear (Wattoma) (active 1860s), Northern Arapaho chief, led his band
during the Powder River Expedition of 1865 and the War for the Bozeman
Trail of 1866–1868. In 1865 his band was defeated at the Battle of Tongue
River early in the Plains Indian wars. On the morning of August 29,
around 125 cavalry and 90 Pawnee warriors under General Patrick E.
Connor ambushed Black Bear's camp at the headwaters of the Tongue
River. The Arapaho were forced to retreat northward, but then rallied and
drove the soldiers back to their artillery position near the village. The warriors had to watch from the hills as the soldiers burned their tipis,
including all their belongings, and drove off about a thousand horses. One
of Black Bear's sons was killed in the attack. Black Bear then allied with the
Sioux, led by Red Cloud, in the War for the Bozeman Trail, which raged
for the next two years.

Left Hand (Nawat, Niwat) (about 1840–1911), Southern Arapaho chief,
tried to keep his people out of the Cheyenne-Arapaho War, also known as
the Colorado War of 1864–1865. His Arapaho band was camped with
Black Kettle's Cheyenne band at Sand Creek in November 1864, when
they were attacked by soldiers under John Chivington. Refusing to fight
back, Left Hand stood defiantly, with his arms folded, and was wounded
nonetheless. After the massacre many of Left Hand's warriors became
hostile despite his determined efforts for peace. When Little Raven died in
1889, Left Hand became principal chief of the Southern Arapaho. In the
ensuing years, he often traveled to Washington, D.C., for lobbying efforts
and various negotiations. Despite the opposition of Arapaho and
Cheyenne tribal members, in 1890 he signed the allotment agreement for
reservation land in Indian Territory (Oklahoma). However, his ability to
compromise did smooth the transition to reservation life for his people.

Left Hand

Little Raven (Hosa) (about 1820–1889), Southern Arapaho chief, was born along the Platte River in what is now Nebraska. He distinguished himself in battles against Sac and Fox warriors, as well as other native people. When his father died in 1855, he became principal chief of the Southern Arapaho. An advocate of peace with settlers, he signed the Fort Wise Treaty of 1861. However, during the Civil War years (1861–1865), he took part in several raids in Colorado and Kansas because of encroachment on Arapaho territory. When Left Hand and his band joined Black Kettle and the Southern Cheyenne at Sand Creek, Little Raven led his people south of the Arkansas River, because he did not trust Colorado Governor John Evans or Colonel John Chivington. Little Raven signed the Little Arkansas Treaties of 1865 and the Medicine Lodge Treaty of 1867, which established the Cheyenne and Arapaho Reservation in Oklahoma. In 1871 he toured several eastern states with other chiefs, and he became well known for his ability as a public speaker. He managed to keep most of his warriors from participating in the Red River War of 1874–1875, which included their Comanche, Kiowa, and Southern Cheyenne allies. Left Hand became chief when Little Raven died in 1889.

Sweezy, Carl (1879–1953), Southern Arapaho artist, began drawing and painting with watercolors when he was a child in Oklahoma. When he was twenty, Sweezy was hired to provide information about Arapaho and Cheyenne traditions to James Mooney, anthropologist at the Smithsonian Institution. Mooney subsequently asked him to restore designs on shields and other artifacts and encouraged the young artist to pursue his distinctive style of painting. Sweezy continued painting while he was working with Mooney, then retired in 1920 to dedicate himself completely to his art. In his work Sweezy depicted traditional activities, such as buffalo hunting, battles on horseback, and religious ceremonies, along with portraits of individuals. His paintings of the Sun Dance are regarded as the best early visual documents of this important ritual, including regalia and

Little Raven

Carl Sweezy

sacred objects. His work has been widely exhibited, and his paintings have been added to the collections of major museums, including the National Museum of the American Indian, University of Oklahoma Museum of Art, and the Oklahoma Historical Society Museum.

Glossary

agent   A Bureau of Indian Affairs employee responsible for U.S. government programs on reservations.

allotment   The nineteenth-century U.S. government policy of dividing tribal lands into small tracts owned by individuals. Also, one of the tracts.

breechcloth   A cloth or skin worn between the legs; also breechclout.

buckskin   Animal hide softened by a tanning or curing process.

buffalo chips   Dried buffalo droppings, which the Arapaho and other Plains Indians used for fuel.

gaqutit   Popular Arapaho guessing game. Also called the hand game.

Ghost Dance   A fervent religious movement that swept the Great Plains in the 1800s, in which people believed that settlers would vanish and the traditional ways would return if people danced and performed certain rituals.

giveaway   A popular ceremony of many Plains tribes, including the Arapaho, in which families offer gifts in honor of a relative, to express appreciation, or to accept a new responsibility.

Great Plains   A vast area of prairie stretching across the North American heartland from Texas to Canada.

lodge   Sacred society whose members sought spiritual power and respect, often by serving the tribe.

Man-Above   Creator of the universe.

massacre   The slaughter of a large number of people.

moccasins   Soft leather shoes, often decorated with brightly colored beads.

Offerings Lodge   A ceremony in which people danced continually for several days until they had visions. Also known as the Sun Dance, or Medicine Lodge.

parfleches   Rawhide pouches for storing food and belongings.

pemmican   Pounded dry meat mixed with fat and berries; used as "energy food" when warriors went on long journeys.

reservation   A tract of land set aside by the government as a home for a Native American tribe.

scalp   A lock of hair and skin from the head of a defeated enemy.

shaman   A holy man or woman who is responsible for the spiritual and physical healing of tribal members.

Sun Dance   Sacred ceremony held every summer in which the Arapaho gave thanks for their good fortune.

sweat lodge   A dome-shaped hut covered with buffalo skins in which purifications and other sacred ceremonies are held.

tipi   Cone-shaped home made of poles covered with animal skins.

travois   A sled made of two poles lashed together and pulled by a dog or horse.

treaty   A signed legal agreement between two nations.

tribal council   The legal governing body for the Arapaho reservation.

warbonnets   Feathered headdresses worn by many Plains warriors, but not traditionally by the Arapaho.

Further Information

The following books were consulted in the research and writing of *The Arapaho*. The two stories included in the text were adapted from tales collected by George A. Dorsey and Alfred L. Kroeber and published in *Traditions of the Arapaho Collected under the Auspices of the Field Columbian Museum and of the American Museum of Natural History*, Chicago, 1903.

Readings

Anderson, Jeffrey D. *The Four Hills of Life: Northern Arapaho Knowledge and Life Movement*. Lincoln: University of Nebraska Press, 2001.

Bass, Althea, Carl Sweezy, and Frank Waters. *The Arapaho Way: A Memoir of an Indian Boyhood*. New York, C.N. Potter, 1966.

Berthrong, Donald J. *The Cheyenne and Arapaho Ordeal: Reservation and Agency Life in the Indian Territory, 1875–1907*. Norman, OK: University of Oklahoma Press, 1992.

Buecker, Thomas R. and R. Eli Paul. *The Crazy Horse Surrender Ledger*. Lincoln, NE: Nebraska State Historical Society, 1994.

Collins, Hubert E. *Storm and Stampede on the Chisholm*. Lincoln, NE: University of Nebraska Press, 1998.

———. *Warpath and Cattle Trail*. Niwot, CO: University Press of Colorado, 1998.

Coel, Margaret. *Chief Left Hand, Southern Arapaho*. Norman, OK: University of Oklahoma Press, 2002.

Coolidge, Grace and George Cornell. *Teepee Neighbors*. Norman, OK: University of Oklahoma Press, 1984.

Densmore, Frances. *Cheyenne and Arapaho Music*. Los Angeles: Southwest Museum, 1964.

Dodge, Richard Irving. *The Indian Territory Journals of Colonel Richard Irving Dodge*. Norman, OK: University of Oklahoma Press, 2000.

Dorsey, George Amos. The Arapaho Sun Dance: The Ceremony of the Offerings Lodge. Millwood, NY: Kraus Reprint Co., 1973.

————. *Traditions of the Arapaho*. Lincoln, NE: University of Nebraska Press, 1998.

Dunn, William R. *"I Stand by Sand Creek": A Defense of Colonel John M. Chivington and the Third Colorado Cavalry*. Fort Collins, CO: Old Army Press, 1985.

Encyclopedia of North American Indians. Tarrytown, NY: Marshall Cavendish, 1997.

Farlow, Edward J. *Wind River Adventures: My Life in Frontier Wyoming*. Glendo, WY: High Plains Press, 1998.

Ferrin, Ida Davison. *Many Moons Ago*. Lake, CO: Filter Press, 1976.

Fowler, Loretta. "Arapaho," *Handbook of North American Indians,* (William C. Sturtevant, general editor), vol. 13: Plains (Raymond J. DeMallie, volume editor), Washington, D.C.: Smithsonian, 2001, pp. 840–862.

————. *Tribal Sovereignty and the Historical Imagination: Cheyenne-Arapaho Politics*. Lincoln, NE: University of Nebraska Press, 2002.

Hilger, M. Inez. *Arapaho Child Life and Its Cultural Background*. Washington, D.C.: U.S. Govt. Print. Off., 1952.

Hoig, Stan. *Fort Reno and the Indian Territory Frontier*. Fayetteville, AR: University of Arkansas Press, 2000.

Johansen, Bruce E., and Donald A. Grinde Jr. *The Encyclopedia of Native American Biography*. New York: Henry Holt and Co., 1997.

Kroeber, A. L. *The Arapaho*. Lincoln, NE: University of Nebraska Press, 1983.

———. *Arapaho Dialects*. Berkeley: University of California Press, 1916.

———. *Decorative Symbolism of the Arapaho*. New York: G.P. Putnam's Sons, 1901.

Malinowski, Sharon. *Notable Native Americans*. Detroit: Gale Research, 1995.

Malinowski, Sharon, and Anna Sheets. *The Gale Encyclopedia of Native American Tribes*. Detroit: Gale Research, 1998.

Mann, Henrietta. *Cheyenne-Arapaho Education, 1871–1982*. Niwot, CO: University Press of Colorado, 1997.

O'Gara, Geoffrey. *What You See in Clear Water: Life on the Wind River Reservation*. New York: Alfred Knopf, 2000.

Penoi, Charles Roderick. *No More Buffaloes*. Yukon, OK: Pueblo Pub. Press, 1984.

Pritzker, Barry M. *Native Americans: An Encyclopedia of History, Culture, and Peoples*. Santa Barbara, CA: ABC-CLIO, 1998.

Salzmann, Zdenek. *The Arapaho Indians: A Research Guide and Bibliography*. New York: Greenwood Press, 1988.

Seger, John H. *Early Days among the Cheyenne and Arapahoe Indians*. Norman, OK: University of Oklahoma Press, 1979.

Trenholm, Virginia Cole. *The Arapahoes, Our People*. Norman, OK: University of Oklahoma Press, 1986.

Children's Books

Fowler, Loretta. *The Arapaho*. New York: Chelsea House Publishers, 1989.

Haluska, Vicki. *The Arapaho Indians*. New York: Chelsea House Publishers, 1993.

Lassieur, Allison. *The Arapaho Tribe*. Mankato, MN: Bridgestone Books, 2002.

Robinson, Maudie. *Grass Singing, Indian Bride of Kit Carson*. Fort Worth, TX: Western Heritage Press, 1977.

Taylor, C. J. *The Ghost and Lone Warrior: An Arapaho Legend*. Toronto: Tundra Books, 1998.

Organizations

Arapaho Business Council
P. O. Box 217
Ft. Washakie, WY 82514
Phone: (307) 332-6120
Fax: (307) 332-7543

Cheyenne and Arapaho Tribes of Oklahoma
P. O. Box 38
Concho, OK 73022
Phone: (405) 262-0345
Fax: (405) 262-0745

Saint Stephen's Indian Mission
30 Saint Stephens Road
Saint Stephens, WY 82524
Phone: (307) 856-7806
Fax: (307) 857-1802

Web Sites

Arapaho
http://www.anthro.mankato.msus.edu/cultural/northamerica/arapaho.html

Arapaho
http://homepages.tesco.net/~richard.alonzo/Tribes/arapaho.htm

Arapaho Business Council
http://tlc.wtp.net/arapaho.htm

Arapaho Literature
http://www.indians.org/welker/arapaho.htm

The Arapaho Project
http://www.colorado.edu/FRIT/arapaho/

The Arapaho Tribe
http://www.omaha.lib.ne.us/transmiss/congress/arapaho.html

Cheyenne and Arapaho Tribes of Oklahoma
http://www.cheyenne-arapaho.org

The Cheyenne and Arapaho Nation
http://users.aol.com/Donh523/navapage/cheyarap.htm

Imaging and Imagining the Ghost Dance
http://php.indiana.edu/~tkavanag/visual5.html

Northern Arapaho Tribe
http://www.northernarapaho.com

The National Parks Service Sand Creek Massacre Project
http://www.sandcreek.org/Massacre/

Notes from "The North American Indian" by E. S. Curtis: Vol. 6, The Arapaho
http://curtis-collection.com/tribe%20data/arapaho.html

The Wyoming Companion (Stories of the Arapaho People)
http://www.wyomingcompanion.com/wcwrr.html

Index

Page numbers in **boldface** are illustrations.

Raymond Bial

HAS PUBLISHED MORE THAN THIRTY CRITICALLY ACCLAIMED BOOKS OF PHOTO-graphs for children and adults. His photo-essays for children include *Corn Belt Harvest, Amish Home, Frontier Home, Shaker Home, The Underground Railroad, Portrait of a Farm Family, With Needle and Thread: A Book About Quilts, Mist Over the Mountains: Appalachia and Its People, Cajun Home,* and *Where Lincoln Walked.*

He is currently immersed in writing *Lifeways,* a series of books about Native Americans. As with his other work, Bial's deep feeling for his subjects is evident in both the text and illustrations. He travels to tribal cultural centers, photographing homes, artifacts, and sur-roundings and learning firsthand about the national lifeways of these peoples.

A full-time library director at a small college in Champaign, Illinois, he lives with his wife and three children in nearby Urbana.